Original title:
Snowy Sleigh Rides and Starlit Skies

Copyright © 2024 Creative Arts Management OÜ
All rights reserved.

Author: Harris Montgomery
ISBN HARDBACK: 978-9916-90-884-6
ISBN PAPERBACK: 978-9916-90-885-3

Northern Lights Keep Watch Over Our Voyage

Bouncing high on fluffy white,
We lose our hats, what a sight!
The reindeer giggle, oh what fun,
As we race beneath the sun.

A snowball flies, it lands with a splat,
Right on the nose of our old cat,
She hisses back, then gives us a glare,
But her fur is now a frosty flair.

Through frosty trails, we sway and slide,
Hot cocoa spills, oh what a ride!
With every turn, laughter erupts,
Even the snowmen dance, sort of clumped.

The stars above wink, a cheeky tease,
As we zoom past the frozen trees,
Our giggles echo, a merry sound,
This winter joy knows no bound!

The Dance of Winter's Breath

A jolly, plump fellow, he slipped on the ice,
With a hoot and a holler, oh, wasn't it nice?
His hat flew away like a bird in a fright,
As he tumbled and rolled through the crisp, chilly night.

His friends all were laughing, they rolled on the ground,
While the moonbeams were laughing without making a sound.
A chorus of giggles, a harmonized cheer,
The dance of winter brought everyone near.

Frost-Kissed Thrills Beneath the Night

On a hillside all frosted, they zipped and they zoomed,
With sleds made of laughter, their spirits were groomed.
'Twas a race down the slope, with a splash and a shout,
And one cheeky fellow rolled right out and about!

His pants got caught on a branch, oh dear!
With a tug and a yank, he yelled, "Don't you dare!"
They pulled and they tugged, what a frosty affair,
While snowflakes were chuckling, and danced in the air.

Celestial Carriages in December

A giant old reindeer played tricks in the night,
He glided on rooftops, a marvelous sight.
With a wink and a nudge, he'd twinkle his nose,
Then swoop down below, where the laughter arose.

"Come join me!" he bellowed, his eyes full of glee,
"We'll prance through the stars, just you wait and see!"
So off they all went, for a whimsical flight,
With giggles and wobbles, they soared through the night.

Glimmers of Hope in Frozen Air

In a town doused in glitter, they gathered with cheer,
For a snowman contest, it was that time of year!
One snowman had gloves that were far too large,
His carrot nose crooked, oh, what a barrage!

With scarves full of colors, they slipped and they fell,
As they fashioned and shaped him, they laughed oh so well.
Then the snowman stood tall, with a goofy old grin,
Spreading warmth through the frost; let the fun now begin!

Dreamy Drifts Under a Canopy of Stars

In a quirky sled, we start to glide,
With hot cocoa spills, oh what a ride!
Laughter erupts as we miss that bend,
'Tis the season to bumble, my friend!

The moon winks down, a comical sight,
As snowballs fly, we take to flight.
Our hats fall off, a chase begins,
Winter mischief, where fun never ends!

Frosted Wishes in the Night's Embrace

With woofs and howls, the dogs take the lead,
Chasing their tails, oh, what a breed!
A snowman blinks, or so it seems,
Could it be magic or just our dreams?

A mishap happens, we trip and roll,
Landing in a snowdrift, heart and soul.
Giggles erupt as we struggle to rise,
This frosted adventure is quite the surprise!

Celestial Glows and Chiming Bells

Bells start jingling, oh what a sound,
As we race through the night, a whirl around!
A hotdog vendor's cart comes into view,
We'll grab some snacks, it's what we do!

As we munch on treats, the stars start to laugh,
We spill our drinks in a playful gaff.
Yet through all the chaos, joy fills the air,
In this winter wonderland, fun is quite rare!

Ethereal Expeditions on Winter's Breath

With every glide, we giggle and shout,
Finding new paths, we wander about.
A tree branch waves as we zoom on by,
"Did it just wave?" we ask with a sigh.

The frost sparkles bright, like glitter on snow,
Each turn we take, brings laughter and glow.
Oops, there goes another flake in my nose,
This chilly escapade is the best, I suppose!

The Lullaby of Snowflakes and Stars

Oh look, a snowball fight, what a sight,
We dodged and weaved with all our might.
But then I slipped, went down with a thud,
Covered in snow, like a big fluffy bud.

The stars overhead are winking bright,
While we roast marshmallows in the moonlight.
One flew too close, it stuck in my hair,
Now I'm a treat that we all can share!

Starry Shadows on Crisp White

With shadows dancing in the cold,
A snowman's hat that's far too bold.
He tips right over, what a funny chap,
And we all laugh, in winter's lap.

The moon peeks down, with a grin so wide,
As we glide on ice, on a magical ride.
But then I twirl and fall on my back,
And all our giggles create a joyful crack!

Journeys of Joy in Winter Darkness

Off we go, through the chilly night,
With hiccups and laughter, everything's light.
The hot cocoa spills, what a sticky fate,
But we swear it's still delicious, taste-tested straight!

Tangled in scarves, all colors and hues,
We can't tell which way is which, just like clues.
But silliness reigns, our hearts are so bright,
As we chase our dreams in this frosty delight!

Beneath the Stars: A Frosted Reverie

Beneath a blanket of shiny white,
We built a fort, oh what a sight!
But the roof collapsed, with a flurry of fun,
Now we're all underneath, soaking up the sun.

Sipping hot chocolate, we spot a deer,
It prances by, oh dear, oh dear!
We wiggle our toes, since they're frozen tight,
As we giggle and dance in the frosty night.

Enchanted Journeys Beneath the Frost

In the chill of the night, we glide,
With laughter like bells, we slide.
Icicles dangle from trees,
As we dodge the cold drafts with ease.

Our hats fly off, what a sight!
Zooming past, oh what delight!
Frosty beards on grinning pals,
Chasing snowflakes, we sound like owls.

A marshmallow fight erupts in glee,
With sticky hands, we shout, "Yippee!"
The snowman tips over, oh my!
We can't stop laughing, oh how we fly!

With cocoa mugs in hand, we cheer,
For all the mishaps, we hold dear.
Under the twinkling, biting frost,
These enchanted nights never feel lost.

Celestial Chariots and Whispers of Joy

On glittering lanes, we race away,
Chariots of laughter, what a display.
With chicken hats and mismatched mitts,
We dodge through snow with clumsy skits.

The stars above twinkle with glee,
As crumbs from cookies cling to me.
We munch and crunch as we glide past,
Hoping these moments will forever last.

Sliding off paths, we hurriedly swerve,
While chasing cosmic sweets we reserve.
The moon chuckles at our wild spree,
"Look at those fools!" says the sky with glee.

Through whispers of joy, we cheer and plight,
As stars wink at our silly fight.
With smiles aglow in the frosty air,
We'll laugh and drum up memories rare.

A Midnight Dance on Icy Highways

Under the moon, our joy ignites,
In prancing boots, we take our flights.
With a flip and a dash, we glide to the beat,
Stealing kisses from frosty treats.

The icicles jive, they twist and sway,
As we bust a move in magical play.
Each slip and slide turns into a blast,
New moves invented, through giggles amassed.

With flurries dancing all around,
We twirl and glide without a sound.
In a tangle of scarves and hats askew,
We get tangled up, in a snowy review.

Our midnight dance has all the flair,
With rhymes of laughter filling the air.
And as we stumble, we just can't care,
For silly memories, these are rare!

Twilight Trails and Twinkling Dreams

Down glowing paths, we zip and zoom,
With cheer that brightens the cold, dark gloom.
The stars above giggle with grace,
As we race ahead, laughter on our face.

In a comedy of errors, we spin and twirl,
Snowballs and giggles in a playful whirl.
We nearly topple from glee and surprise,
As friendly snowmen roll back their eyes.

The magic of twilight fills our hearts,
Tickling our feet, as the fun all starts.
With big, fluffy hats and socks gone astray,
Who knew a night could feel this way?

Gripping our cocoa, we sing out loud,
In this winter wonderland, we are proud.
With twinkling stars as our guiding beams,
We'll float through this night in whimsical dreams.

Enchanted Rides Beneath Celestial Canopies

As we bounce along the trail,
The reindeer dance, they tell a tale.
Hot cocoa spills, we laugh and shout,
Who knew the night would be this bout?

Snowflakes swirl, a frosty show,
Lost a mitten? Where did it go?
With every bump, we squeal and cheer,
This ride's a riot, that much is clear.

Stars above are winking bright,
They giggle softly at our flight.
Our hats are askew, laughter's our guide,
What a joy to ride this wild slide!

Under the moon's mischievous grin,
We plot our course, let the fun begin!
Hearts alight with joyous cheer,
What a silly, wondrous year!

Twilight Adventures on Crystal Ways

The bells go jingle, what a sound,
We race on paths, no solid ground.
Jim's lost his scarf, it flutters free,
Is that really just a squirrel we see?

Wobbling, tumbling through the night,
A hot dog stand? What a delight!
We'll stop for snacks, it's only fair,
With ketchup flies through icy air!

Giggles rise like snowflakes fall,
We chase each other, then we stall.
My nose is red, my cheeks are too,
The twinkling lights spell out 'Yoo-hoo!'

As we glide beneath the stars,
Who knew we'd travel near and far?
We're off again, with one last cheer,
The best adventure of the year!

A Serenade of Wind and Whispers

The wind it whistles, oh so loud,
We zoom past trees, we've made a crowd.
Stan lost his hat, now what a fluke,
It's perched upon a passing stork!

In the crisp air, we start to sing,
Our voices echo, what joy they bring.
But who keeps hitting me with snow?
Was it Fred or his throwing elbow?

Round the bend, what do I see?
A raccoon dancing, happy and free.
We raise a toast with icy drinks,
To silly moments, pause and winks!

With starlight twinkling, giggles soar,
Our hearts are light, we're wanting more.
An adventure built on friendship's cheer,
What a way to spend the year!

Crystalline Trails of Evening Magic

On a winter's night, we take a ride,
The laughter echoes far and wide.
Tripping through the leaves, oh dear,
Someone's sock has disappeared!

With blankets bunched and cheeks so red,
A fierce snowball soon will be fed.
But watch your aim, oh what a shot,
Did I just hit the candy hotpot?

Around we tumble, laughter bright,
Our glowing cheeks reflect the night.
The stars above can't help but joke,
As we get tangled in a cloak!

So here we glide, all in good fun,
This wild ride has only begun.
With tales to tell and memories spun,
Who knew winter could be this pun?

The Whisper of Reindeer in the Night

When reindeer dance upon the roof,
They giggle and snort, oh what a hoot!
With jingle bells tinkling in delight,
They take off like rockets into the night.

Under the moon, they slip and slide,
With antlers entangled, they laugh and glide.
A game of tag on the frosty beams,
Chasing their dreams, or so it seems.

Cookies are missing, what a surprise!
Caught in the act, with wide-open eyes.
They munch and crunch with mischievous cheer,
As they frolic about, spreading good cheer.

So if you hear a ruckus above,
Just know it's reindeer spreading their love.
With laughter and joy, they soar through the night,
Bringing giggles and glee, oh what a sight!

Velvet Nights and Airy Flights

In plush evenings where dreams take flight,
We leap on sleds with all our might.
Through fluffy hills, we zoom and glide,
Spinning around like a rollercoaster ride.

With hot cocoa splashed down our coats,
We tumble and roll, oh how we gloat!
The wind in our hair, those glimmers of fun,
Our cheeks are rosy, our laughter spun.

Under the stars, we race and race,
Imagining ourselves in a wild goose chase.
With snowballs flying, we make our stand,
Trying to dodge what we cannot withstand.

Each snowy drift, a giggle fest,
Tumbling and tripping, we never rest.
Velvet nights filled with playful glee,
Oh, how we cherish our youthful spree!

Echoes of Laughter in Frost-Kissed Air

With frosty noses and cheeks aglow,
The sound of our laughter starts to flow.
We build a snowman, tall and round,
With a carrot nose that tumbles down.

In frozen fields, we challenge our fate,
Sliding and crashing, oh isn't it great?
Every slip, a comical fall,
Yet laughter echoes, we're having a ball.

The snowballs whizz past like playful darts,
With squeals and shouts, we play our parts.
"Not in my hair!" we squeal with delight,
As we pelt each other, full of good fright.

Frost-kissed air filled with mirthful cheer,
Memories made that seem so near.
In the chill of the night, we're warm inside,
As echoes of laughter our hearts do guide.

Winter's Canvas, Painted with Starlight

Under a blanket of shimmering white,
We dot the landscape, what a sight!
With laughter and giggles, the world is bright,
Like whimsical artists, creating our flight.

We toss snow like painter's brush,
Swirls of white in a glorious hush.
With twinkling stars, our canvas so grand,
Crafting snow creations with a gentle hand.

The snow angel's wings, oh what a surprise,
With giggles and flair, we paint the skies.
Each little flake tells a silly tale,
As we come together, we'll never fail.

In winter's embrace, with joy so rife,
We find our fun, our laughter, our life.
So here's to the nights where memories gleam,
Painting starlit wonders, living the dream!

Celestial Carriage Through Crisp Air

In a basket of blankets, we cheer,
Laughter echoes, we're full of good cheer.
The horse looks bemused, with a snort and a jig,
As we bounce and we giggle, oh what a big wig!

With the stars as our guide, we dance through the night,
Chasing the moonbeams with laughter and light.
The carriage goes bump, like a ride on the sea,
Drifting through laughter, oh just wait and see!

Frosty Hooves and Glimmering Night

With hooves like ice skates and a twinkle of glee,
We zip through the woods, just as fast as can be.
The reins in my hands, but the horse takes the lead,
While I brace for the bumps and a snow-laden creed.

Bells jingle in rhythm, like a clumsy parade,
We spin through the drifts, oh what a charade!
The cocoa is spilling, oh where did it go?
Hot drinks in the air, a frosty fray show!

Riding the Silk of Silent Slumber

The night gently whispers, the air starts to freeze,
As the wheels of our carriage hum sweetly like bees.
I spot a small rabbit, he's dancing with flair,
With a hop and a skip; oh, do we dare stare?

We glide past the trees, under branches that creak,
The stars do a shimmy, a cosmic sneak peek.
Yet my hat starts to sway, as the wind goes still,
Catching laughter like snowflakes, oh what a thrill!

Starlight Serenades on a Frozen Path

With a wink at the cosmos, my heart starts to soar,
As we thread through the night, it's a magical chore.
A snowball skirmish completes our delight,
While the horse rolls his eyes, oh, what a sight!

We sing off-key tunes, a harmonious mess,
Surrounded by twinkle, we couldn't care less.
The cold can't dampen our joy and our fun,
As we celebrate life 'til the rise of the sun!

Midnight Magic Under a Tapestry of Light

In frosty air, we slipped and slid,
Caught a snowball—who threw that bid?
The lamp post winked, the stars did grin,
As we raced the cat, but she just pinned.

Mittens tangled, laughter loud,
Our trusty steed? A squirrel was proud!
With jingles ringing from every toe,
Who knew that snow could steal the show?

Sleds turned sideways, giggles high,
We floated past, oh my, oh my!
A snowman waved with carrot nose,
Did we just pass? Who really knows!

Under skies so bright, we danced and twirled,
Finding treasure in every swirl.
Midnight magic held us tight,
In this blizzard, we found our light.

Moonbeams and Maplewood Melodies

With moonbeams weaving through the trees,
We sledded past some bumblebees.
They buzzed along our tuneful song,
While we giggled at their buzzing throng.

A maple tree leaned down to say,
'Take a ride, it's a perfect day!'
So off we went, what a glorious sight,
With choirs of owls joining our flight.

Our hats blew off, but spirits were high,
As pinecones fell from the canopy sky.
Chasing memories like cats in a race,
In this sweet chaos, we found our place.

From gliding paths to frosty laughs,
Each turn we took carved new paragraphs.
In moonlit glades, our hearts took wing,
In this harmony, we felt everything!

Gliding Through the Galaxy of Snow

With our trusty sled, we took a leap,
Past the trees, and into the deep.
Stars above were twinkling so bright,
While we tumbled down, causing pure delight.

A snowman chuckled, adjusting his scarf,
Telling us jokes we couldn't help but laugh.
The frosty breeze joined in the cheer,
As snowflakes rapped on our ears, so near.

We twirled and spun, a cosmic ballet,
With hot cocoa dreams at the end of the day.
Soaring high through the wintery night,
Our laughter echoed—it felt so right.

As we glided along, time danced away,
The moon played host to our wild ballet.
In a whimsy world where fun never slows,
We floated forever in the galaxy of snow.

Harmonies of the Night: A Ride in Time

The clock struck two as we hit the hill,
With a splat and a giggle—and oh, what a thrill!
Mittens flew while we raced with glee,
Who knew the night could be so carefree?

Raccoons joined, in tuxedos they pranced,
Shimmied along as they took their chance.
In moonlit rhythm, we found our beat,
As snowflakes danced, oh what a treat!

The toboggan squeaked like a glamorous car,
We revved up joy, our own shining star.
And if you ask, "What's the best part?"
It's sharing a twirl with a snow-covered heart.

With echoes of laughter and magical sights,
We wrote our own songs on those chilly nights.
In harmony discovered, and melody divine,
We rode through the mist, a moment in time.

The Glow of Lanterns in Winter's Chill

In winter's grasp, we glide and sway,
With lanterns bright, we light the way.
The ice cracks loud, a quirky sound,
As laughter echoes all around.

Hot cocoa spills on my favorite hat,
While snowflakes dance like a fluffy cat.
We race and trip, oh what a sight,
In this chilly fun, we find delight.

The snowmen grin with carrot smiles,
As we tumble over, in playful piles.
With mittens tangled, hands in a twist,
Adventure awaits, none can resist.

So gather 'round, let's warm the night,
With silly stories and frosty bites.
Under the glow, our spirits soar,
In winter's chill, who could ask for more?

Celestial Choreography in December

The stars above begin to twirl,
As we dance on ice, give a whirl.
My boots go left, oh no, they slide,
I twirl and pitch, what a wild ride!

Comets zoom as we laugh and gasp,
While hot hands warm the cocoa clasp.
With snowball fights, we wage our wars,
The moon just chuckles, how time soars!

Frosty patterns on our rosy cheeks,
As we improvise our silly peaks.
With every leap, a giggle flies,
Under this sky, oh how time pries!

So hear, my friend, the frosty chords,
Of winter's tunes and icy swords.
With every slip, we find our beat,
In December's dance, oh, nothing's fleet!

Moonbeams and Whispers of Adventure

As moonbeams play with frosted trees,
We waddle forth with a joyous tease.
The snowflakes tickle noses and toes,
While hot drinks spill on fuzzy clothes.

We climb aboard a wooden throne,
With dreamers' tales and laughter grown.
Each hill we crest, a new surprise,
As starlit dreams fill up the skies.

Clumsily sliding, we tip and sway,
The night alights, in a dazzling way.
The owls hoot sage advice, so wise,
While we perform our clumsy highs!

Through frosty paths, we roam and squeal,
With daring hearts, we spin and wheel.
Adventure's call, oh how it sings,
In moonlit realms, we're all like kings!

The Frosty Canvas of Night's Embrace

The night unveils its frosty art,
As we embark, let fun impart.
With every step, a soundtrack sings,
Of chuckling winds and funny flings.

We paint the snow with silly tales,
With footprints that tell of snowbound gales.
Did I just trip or do a dance?
In this crazy night, we take a chance!

A festive crew, we hoot and cheer,
As goofy antics fill the air.
The stars giggle, the moon winks bright,
In our frosty canvas, joy takes flight.

So let's create this winter's fun,
With laughter echoing, one by one.
In the embrace of night's delight,
We find our joy, the world feels right!

The Art of Winter Whispers

Beneath the frosty moon's embrace,
We ride with cheeky smiles of grace.
Reindeer prance and snowballs fly,
Laughter echoes, oh my, oh my!

Hot cocoa spills like secret dreams,
As we plot our next mischievous schemes.
Slippery slopes, we tumble and roll,
Cape of snow gives us all a goal!

Whispers of snowmen in the glade,
Wink at us as we start our parade.
Each flap of the sleigh's jolly cheer,
Leaves us giggling year after year!

Through frosty breath, a snowball fight,
With every throw, we gain new height.
The art of fun on a chilly night,
In winter's wonder, all feels just right!

Frosty Adventures Beneath a Sea of Stars

We zip and zoom beneath shining lights,
Careening past owls with wild delight.
Elves on skates zoom by in a whirl,
As we snicker and watch snowflakes twirl!

Hot sleds crashing—what a sight!
With giggles echoing into the night.
Snowmen frown when we call them names,
But who can resist these silly games?

A snowball brigade takes its aim,
But laughter drowns out their blunt claim.
Round the bend, we hit a stash,
Of twinkling lights in a frosty flash!

Underneath a quilt of cold and bright,
The stars dance with our sheer delight.
Warming hearts even in the freeze,
Together we frolic, forever at ease!

Midnight Rambles Through Silvered Woods

The woods sparkles with mischief anew,
What's that sneaky squirrel up to?
He's plotting a heist for the acorn stash,
While our sleigh glides with a joyous crash!

We race with owls, oh what a sight!
Chasing the moon in the shimmery night.
With each twist and turn, we belt out tunes,
While dancing with shadows in glowing dunes!

Frosty breath blending in the air,
A snowball hurls, but we don't care.
We giggle and tumble, a fumble, a fall,
Each echoing laugh is the best gift of all!

Through silvered woods and playful trees,
We'll ride 'til dawn, if you please.
Midnight rambles with hearts set free,
Chasing wonders where glee's the decree!

Enigmas of the Night in Winter's Hold

In the grip of winter's witty embrace,
Mysteries dance at a frosty pace.
Every corner hides a prank or jest,
Oh, the joy is at its very best!

Sleds collide in an accidental cheer,
As giggles spread from ear to ear.
The moon naps low, a watchful guide,
While woodland creatures laugh and glide!

What's that rustling? Just a raccoon?
Fashioned in snow with a dash of tune.
With hiccups of laughter to fill the night,
In winter's hold, everything feels right!

So here's to the mysteries we cherish,
Through whimsical trails that never perish.
In frosty fun, we forever revolve,
Each enigma, a joke we solve!

Dances of Light in the Frosty Air

In the chill, we wiggle and cheer,
With mittens that will disappear.
Our toes are frozen, yet we prance,
While snowflakes giggle at our dance.

A snowman winks, what a sight!
His carrot nose seems just too bright.
We twirl around in swirling fun,
As giggles echo, one by one.

The stars join in with winks and spins,
While snowboards fly, oh where to begin?
With hot cocoa as our daring prize,
We toast to winter with silly cries!

So come, my friends, let's have a blast,
With frosty games that will last and last.
Let's build a fort and battle snow,
And laugh until our cheeks are aglow.

Celestial Lanterns Above Drifting Snow

See how the lanterns shine so bright,
While we trip over snowdrifts in flight.
With laughter rising, we glide and slide,
While frozen paws show much canine pride.

Here comes a sled with friends galore,
But wait! What's that?—a fall on the floor!
With giggles that echo all around,
We tumble and roll, no worries found.

The stars above whisper winter's jokes,
As we make snow angels in silly pokes.
Each flake brings laughter, a frosty tease,
In the sparkling night, we do what we please.

So grab your hats and keep your socks,
We'll make snowmen with floppy clocks.
As laughter swirls with frosty air,
We'll forget our worries, without a care.

Tales of Magic in the Moonlight

Beneath the moon, we tell our tales,
Of unicorns and snowy trails.
With hot dogs roasting by the glow,
We laugh at how our hair's got snow!

Oh, look at that, a flying cat!
He's zooming high, where's he at?
But then he lands, a flurry of fur,
And we all giggle, oh what a blur!

A yeti shuffles, can you believe?
His dance moves make us all reprieve.
With jingle bells upon his feet,
We cheer him on, our winter treat.

So gather round, let's spin some yarns,
With silly stories and winter charms.
In the glimmering night, we roam so free,
With laughter bouncing, you'll want to stay and see!

Quiet Secrets on Shimmering Trails

In the hush of night, we tiptoe light,
Whispering secrets, what a sight!
With snowball fights and giggles loud,
The critters scurry, oh so proud.

A fox in a scarf prances by,
With twinkling eyes like stars on high.
As we sneak 'round with mischief gleams,
We burst into laughter, almost screams.

But oh, beware the puddles near,
They hide their tricks without any fear!
With splashes and slips, we all collapse,
As snowflakes flutter like playful laps.

So let's weave through the icy land,
Chasing the moon like a merry band.
With love and laughter, we stomp and sway,
In our winter wonderland, forever we play.

The Mosaic of Frigid Dreams

A jolly crew in coats so bright,
Tumbled down in pure delight.
Their laughter flies on icy breeze,
While snowflakes dance among the trees.

With cocoa mugs, they spill the tea,
A snowball fight, oh, such glee!
They slip and slide, a wild parade,
Each tumble met with cheers displayed.

A dog in boots upon the scene,
Chasing snowmen, oh so keen.
With scarves on wrong and mittens lost,
Their winter fun, always worth the cost.

Like penguins waddling, they unite,
To make a fort, they squawk and bite.
When evening comes, they gaze above,
At winking stars like gifts of love.

Nimbus of Frost Under a Sea of Light

Bumpy rides on sleds of dreams,
They whoosh down hills, shrill excited screams.
A choo-choo train of laughter flows,
As someone's hat takes flight like crows.

Slippery snacks from pockets tossed,
With every bite, their dignity lost.
A blizzard friend with a carrot nose,
Looks sternly at them as chaos grows.

Each twist and turn, a comic tale,
With giggles spilling like frosty hail.
Up in the air, their troubles flee,
On whimsical winds, they twist with glee.

But now the moon is quite a tease,
The lopsided snowman begins to freeze.
They dash for warmth, with cheeks aglow,
While winter's fun puts on a show.

Twilight Enchantment on Frozen Roads

Gliding through the evening haze,
Unexpected bumps bring silly gaze.
A crew of pals, all puffed and bright,
Slide sideways, laughing at their plight.

In woolly hats that flop about,
They squeal, they slip, but there's no doubt.
With every gust, a joyful cry,
As twinkling lights above them sigh.

A chase ensues with snowflakes thrown,
Accidental snowmen scratches grown.
With cocoa spills and marshmallows missed,
They cheers their way through every twist.

With stars like gumdrops up above,
They craft their stories, sprinkled with love.
As winter night brings frosty mirth,
They spin and roll, for all its worth.

Blessed by the Bounty of Winter's Gleam

A jingle here, a jangle there,
With jingling laughter filling air.
Adventures form like frosty billow,
On pathways curled from frozen willow.

A snowman's kid with lopsided grin,
Hoarding carrots, makes a terrific din.
As friends collide in gentle spree,
Frosty whispers echo garden glee.

Fingers numb, but spirits light,
They dash like reindeer in delight.
With every plop, the giggles grow,
In winter's cozy, glimmering glow.

As moonlight beams and shadows prance,
They join together in a merry dance.
With hearts aglow, they celebrate,
In winter's arms, they feel so great.

Starry Nights and Hoofbeats

Under twinkling stars we fly,
Laughter echoes, oh my, oh my!
With floppy hats and mittens tight,
We bounce and jostle, what a sight!

The horses snort, they leap and prance,
While we fumble, not a chance!
Hot cocoa spills upon my ear,
That chilly drink—bring me some beer!

The moonlight paints our merry crew,
With misadventures, all brand new.
I lost my boot, but who cares now?
I'll ride barefoot, hop like a cow!

With every bump, we laugh and cheer,
What's winter fun without some beer?
Through frosty air we yell and sing,
Oh what jolly joys we bring!

Frosty Romance in a Winter Wonderland

In a frozen land of dreams and cheer,
I waved at you, you waved back, dear!
But while I posed for quite a show,
My nose fell off—from ice too low!

We spun around, a dizzy dance,
You swept me up—oh what romance!
But then you slipped, oh what a sight,
We both went down in pure delight!

Your hat landed on a snowman's head,
"Now that's a look!" I loudly said.
You winked and made a snowball throw,
It hit me hard—oh wait, was that snow?!

In frosty fun, we found our bliss,
A snowy kiss—quite hard to miss!
With laughter ringing through the night,
We danced beneath the stars so bright!

Echoes of Laughter Through the Pines

Whispers tumble through the trees,
Laughter dances on the breeze.
We're bundled up, with cheeks so red,
On frosty trails, our dreams are fed.

A tumble here, a slip or two,
We break the ice, the cold is new!
Your scarf gets stuck; it's quite a show,
You pull and pull, and round we go!

The pines are tall, the night's a hoot,
I swear I saw a four-legged brute!
We chase the shadows, racing fast,
Falling down, we giggle at last!

With echoes ringing, joyful calls,
We fumble through the winter stalls.
As laughter lifts, our hearts grow light,
In nature's hug, we feel just right!

A Tapestry of Snowflakes and Stars

Dancing snowflakes swirl and twirl,
We weave between the frosty whirl.
With laughter bursting, kindness near,
Each shimmering flake feels like a beer!

The sled goes bump, then whips around,
Our giggles echo, such a sound!
Your hat flies off, it arcs so high,
And lands upon a tree nearby!

Mittens clash, while snowballs soar,
A soft white war, oh, we want more!
With sangfroid spirit, we take aim,
Let's see who falls first in this game!

As starlight winks down from above,
We cherish moments—full of love.
In this frosty world, let's make a pact,
To laugh and play—that's a fact!

Whispers of Winter's Embrace

In a frosty land where giggles play,
Snowflakes slip and dance away.
Hot cocoa spills with a silly grin,
As snowmen wobble, the fun begins.

With boots that scare, we stride in style,
Tripping and tumbling, oh, what a trial!
But laughter erupts with every fall,
Like penguins on ice, we prank one and all.

Chase the frostbite, but what a tease,
Frosty noses chill with ease.
Snowballs fly, but we pretend to pout,
The truth is, we can't live without!

Oh, winter's charm is quite a jest,
With each leap and bound, we give our best.
So snuggle up and don your gear,
In this land of folly, we find good cheer.

Starlight on Frosted Paths

Under twinkling lights like frosted dreams,
We stumble and fumble, or so it seems.
With giggles that float on a crispy breeze,
We zip down hills like a pack of bees!

The stars above wink with a gleeful glow,
As sleds collide in a friendly row.
'You missed me!' shouts one, with a laugh and a spin,
While the brave-hearted champion wipes off their chin.

Through forests of snow, we race with glee,
Chasing our shadows, wild and free.
'Think I'm faster?' we giggle and cheer,
But really, it's chaos that draws us near!

Laughter echoes under the moon so bright,
As we tumble and roll, what a joyful sight!
In this sparkling charm, we taste the fun,
With every wiped tear, winter's just begun.

Chasing Dreams Under Glittering Canopies

In the whimsical woods where the critters hide,
We zoom on sleds, no place to bide.
A squirrel takes cover, 'What's this ruckus?'
Rolling in giggles, our joy's contagious!

The moon peeks through like a playful friend,
While snowflakes scatter, with twists they send.
'Catch a comet!' one yells with a grin,
As everyone tumbles and lands in a spin.

The stars above are our watchful crew,
As we build a fort, a grand place to view.
But oh, what's this? An avalanche near,
We laugh till we cry, our spirits sincere!

Under a quilt of dreams and a chilly breeze,
The night blooms with magic, all worries freeze.
Let joy run amok, take the silly ride,
In this world of fancy, we're filled with pride.

Moonlit Journeys on Silent Trails

The moon's an accomplice in our merry spree,
With shadows that dance, wild as can be.
Sleds come a-calling, with wheels of delight,
Through fluffy white hills, we soar in flight.

Whoops and hollers echo through the night,
As we wiggle and jostle, oh, what a sight!
A snowball flies, hitting the mark,
And giggles erupt like sparks in the dark.

We carve up the snow like artists of fun,
Creating a canvas till the morning has run.
Each slip and slide; a comic ballet,
As laughter brings warmth in the chilly array.

With starlit paths knitting dreams that gleam,
We chase after joy, like a daydreaming team.
So here's to the magic, the smiles we find,
In this whimsical winter where fun's intertwined.

Nighttime Revelries in Frosty Splendor

Laughter echoes through the night,
As we slide by with pure delight.
Hot cocoa spills, a marshmallow fight,
Oh, who knew winter could bring such height?

The reindeer dance on frozen lakes,
While penguins plot their icy pranks.
With every laugh, the world awakes,
We're kings and queens, just look at our flanks!

Sleds go flying, hats take flight,
Yelling 'whoa' like it's a fright.
The snowman winks, what a sight,
He's joined our quest, to cheer the night!

We tumble down, and fit our mask,
Of silly gear, an easy task.
With joyful shouts, no time to bask,
Winter's grip, we bravely unmask!

The Poetry of Cold on Velvet Skies

A snowball sneaks behind my ear,
Betrayed by a friend and then I cheer.
The stars are bright, or is that beer?
Let's toast to the night, with holiday cheer!

Frosty fingers, we can't feel,
But let's make snow angels, that's a deal!
With giggles shared, all wounds we heal,
In this winter wonderland, it's surreal!

The moonlight glows, the sled holds tight,
With whirls and twirls, we take our flight.
With every bump, screams of delight,
The world is ours—oh, such a sight!

Instead of drums, we have our thighs,
As we race beneath these glittering skies.
Who knew our laughter could reach such highs?
In frosty realms, we are the spies!

A Starlit Veil Over Frozen Meadows

Whispers of chill wrapped in a hug,
Missed my aim! That snowball bug!
With squeals and shouts, we dance and shrug,
This winter magic, my heart is snug.

Where frosty breath creates the art,
On frozen ground, we play our part.
With every slip, we go for a start,
We find the joy, it's a work of heart!

Gentle flakes on our noses land,
As sledding legends go hand in hand.
We'll toast our toes, it's all been planned,
In laughter's grip, we take a stand!

Each twinkle brightens the chilly dark,
With silly games, we light the park.
With hats askew, our spirits spark,
In this winter night, let's leave a mark!

Portals of Light in the Chilling Dark

Floating down the hills we glide,
With cheeks like roses, from joy we bide.
The stars are our guide, they never hide,
In this frosty haven, come take a ride!

As laughter tumbles from painted lips,
We navigate the icy trips.
Riding high, as friendship dips,
With each snowstorm, the winter grips!

There's magic here in every twist,
Though icy kisses can't be missed.
With silly pranks wrapped in a fist,
Winter nights, oh how they persist!

Under the glow, we share our dreams,
Warming hearts through laughter's beams.
In this chill where whimsy teems,
Forever our fun, or so it seems!

Luminous Dreams in a Frozen Realm

In a land where snowflakes dance and twirl,
A fox in a hat gives a twirl,
His friends all laugh as they glide beside,
On a frozen pond, they can't hide their pride.

A penguin slips, a comical sight,
Waddling hard, oh what a fright!
The stars above are giggling low,
As frostbitten cheeks begin to glow.

Laughter echoes through the crisp air,
Sledding down hills without a care,
With cocoa spills and marshmallow dreams,
This winter fun isn't as it seems.

So grab a friend, let's make a dash,
Through piles of snow, we'll make a splash,
In this realm where winter's here,
Let's spread the joy, bring on the cheer!

A Ride Through Time Beneath the Night

A bumpy start on a wooden sleigh,
We're off to conquer the winter's play,
The reins are tight, oh what a sight,
As plump old reindeer take off in flight.

Behind us trails a snowman's hat,
His carrot nose gave a little pat,
"How rude!" he yells, as we roll on by,
While icicles hang with a frosty sigh.

The stars are winking, sharing a wink,
As we slide and spin, and start to think,
Maybe this ride wasn't thought out well,
When we crash into snowbanks and make quite a swell!

But laughter drowns the winter's cold,
As we spin tales of brave and bold,
With snow in our hair and hearts full of glee,
There's nowhere else we'd rather be!

Adventurous Spirits in the Frosty Glow

With a marshmallow moon bright in the sky,
We set out to see just how high we can fly,
Squeals of delight as we tumble and spin,
Who knew being frosty could be this much fun?

A flurry of giggles, a dash down the hill,
With twirls and twists, we're never still,
Then Oops! A faceplant in frosty whites,
But up I pop, ready for more bites!

The stars look down with a knowing grin,
As we start a snowball fight, let the games begin!
Snowmen become targets, they just can't win,
For joy in our hearts is where we begin.

So grab your mittens, let's run and play,
In this winter wonder, we'll laugh all day,
With twinkling lights and a party on ice,
The magic of winter is quite the surprise!

Winter Whispers in Moonlit Trails

In the hush of night, a whispering breeze,
An owl on a branch watches us with ease,
"Keep it down!" he hoots, as we make a scene,
With laughter and cheer, how merry we've been!

Through powdery paths and trails of delight,
We race one another, all giggles and fright,
Then a snowball flies, oh what a mess,
Now everyone's covered; I must confess!

But who can stay mad in this frosty glow?
When icicles sparkle, and merriment flows,
With cheeks rosy red and hearts full of light,
Our winter escapades fill every night.

So come join the fun, slip on your gear,
Let's blaze through the night without any fear,
For in this realm painted in moonlit cheer,
The laughter we share brings warmth, my dear!

Celestial Vistas and Winter's Caress

As we zoom down the hill, quite the sight,
My hat flies off, oh what a fright!
Laughter spills, we clutch our sides,
In this chilly chaos, joy resides.

Hot cocoa spills, like a winter stream,
"Catch that marshmallow!" becomes the theme.
Slipping and sliding, a comical plight,
A tumble here, a giggle tonight!

The stars twinkle bright, like winking eyes,
While we dodge snowballs under frosty skies.
Our cheeks all rosy, hearts feel so bold,
In this jolly journey, fond memories unfold.

With every turn, our spirits take flight,
A dance with the snowflakes, oh what a night!
We ride on the laughter, let each moment sing,
In the frosty wonder, happiness we bring.

Whispers of Frost on Evergreen Roads

With a jingle and jangle, we dash and sway,
The trees whisper secrets, come join the play!
A catapulted snowman, oh what a sight,
His carrot nose crooked, he's lost his fight!

Down the path, we roll with cheer,
Making snow angels, with laughter near.
Frosty the snowman gives us a shout,
But his voice gets lost in the flurry of clout!

We stumble and tumble, a wonderful mess,
Hats flying off, pure silliness!
The stars overhead, giggling in glee,
As we build a ramp—the funniest spree!

In the glow of moonlight, we glide and swerve,
With dreamy delights, we laugh and observe.
The night holds wonders, oh how they gleam,
In our wintery world, we chase every dream!

Shooting Stars and Winter's Whisper

Through the frosty air, in a cheerful fleet,
We rush on soft snow, it's quite a feat!
Stars above twinkle, like coins in a jar,
"Race you to that bush!"—whoever you are!

With wintery giggles, we take to the lane,
"Whoa!" someone slips in a fluffy terrain.
A chorus of chuckles erupts in the night,
As we tumble like snowflakes, pure delight!

The moon beams down with a smirk on its face,
While we navigate chaos, a sugar-plum race.
The snowman does dance, or so we declare,
As we trip on our laughter, float free in the air!

The twinkling lights, they greet our parade,
Each glimmer a giggle, each sparkle a shade.
With friends all around, and the stars in view,
Our playful adventure feels timeless and new!

Pushing Through Dreams Under Twinkling Lights

In the frosty air, we glide with flair,
The stars like confetti, love's perfect pair.
Twirling and swirling, our laughter ignites,
Under the moon's glow, we embrace the nights.

With mittens all snug, and cheeks cherry bright,
We journey through giggles, embracing the light.
"Catch that cold breeze!" we shout with delight,
As snowflakes fall down, a whimsical flight!

The sled dips and dives, a comical ride,
As we burst into fits, on snow we collide.
The bright light above, like a giggling sprite,
Sprinkles us with joy, so pure and so bright!

Through laughter and dreams, we dash and we cheer,
Each moment a treasure, gathered so dear.
With memories woven from frosty charms,
Together we'll dance, in dreams and in arms!

Milton Keynes UK
Ingram Content Group UK Ltd.
UKHW020047271124
451585UK00012B/1096

9 789916 908853